UNLOCK YOUR POTENTIAL

A Guide to Personal Development and Growth

Mack E. Rogas

Mack E. Rogas

TABLE OF CONTENT

INTRODUCTION

The journey of personal development is a lifelong process of self-discovery and growth. It involves taking deliberate steps towards becoming the best version of ourselves, achieving our goals, and living a fulfilling life.

This book aims to provide you with practical guidance and tips on various aspects of personal development, including goal setting, mindset, time management, self-care, relationships, communication, and continuous learning.

By implementing the strategies outlined in this book, you'll be able to overcome obstacles, improve your productivity, boost your confidence, enhance your relationships, and ultimately achieve your full potential.

Whether you're a seasoned personal development enthusiast or just starting your journey, this book is designed to help you take your first steps towards a more fulfilling and purposeful life. So let's get started!

CHAPTER ONE

WHAT IS PERSONAL DEVELOPMENT?

Personal development is the process of improving oneself through conscious and intentional actions. It involves taking steps to develop new skills, expand knowledge, enhance personality traits, and achieve personal goals.

The goal of personal development is to improve all aspects of one's life, including personal relationships, career, health, and overall well-being. This process requires self-reflection, self-awareness, and a willingness to learn and grow.

Personal development encompasses a wide range of activities, including reading books, attending workshops or courses, practising new habits, setting and achieving goals, seeking feedback, and working on personal strengths and weaknesses.

Ultimately, personal development is about becoming the best version of oneself and living a more fulfilling and purposeful life.

WHY IS PERSONAL DEVELOPMENT IMPORTANT?

Personal development is important for several reasons, including:

1. Increased Self-Awareness: Personal development helps individuals gain a better understanding of themselves, their strengths and weaknesses, and their values and beliefs. This self-awareness allows individuals to make more informed decisions and live more purposeful lives.

2. Improved Self-Confidence: As individuals work on their personal growth, they gain more confidence in

their abilities and become more comfortable with themselves. This increased self-confidence can lead to more success in personal and professional endeavours.

3. Better Relationships: Personal development can help individuals improve their communication skills, become better listeners, and build stronger relationships with others.

4. Increased Resilience: By developing resilience and coping mechanisms, individuals can better handle life's challenges and bounce back from setbacks.

5. Professional Development: Personal development can lead to improved job performance, increased career opportunities, and higher earning potential.

6. Greater Fulfilment: Personal development helps individuals identify their passions and purpose, leading to greater fulfilment and happiness in life.

Overall, personal development is essential for achieving a fulfilling and successful life. It helps individuals grow and become the best version of themselves, leading to better relationships, career success, and personal fulfilment.

HOW THIS BOOK CAN HELP YOU

This book is designed to provide you with practical guidance and tips on various aspects of personal development, including goal setting, mindset, time management, self-care, relationships, communication, and continuous learning.

By reading this book and implementing the strategies outlined, you can:

1. Gain A Better Understanding of Yourself: Self-awareness is the foundation of personal development. By understanding your strengths, weaknesses, values, and beliefs, you can make informed decisions, improve your relationships, and achieve your goals. This book will help you become more self-aware and identify areas for personal growth.

2. Set and Achieve Personal Goals: Goal setting is a powerful tool that can help you focus your energy and efforts. By setting specific, measurable, achievable, relevant, and time-bound (SMART) goals, you can create a roadmap to success and stay motivated throughout the journey. You'll learn how to set

achievable goals and create a plan to achieve them.

3. Improve Your Mindset: Your mindset is your mental attitude and approach to life. By cultivating a growth mindset, which is characterized by a belief that one's abilities can be developed through dedication and hard work, you can overcome obstacles, learn from failures, and achieve your full potential. You'll learn how to cultivate a growth mindset and overcome limiting beliefs.

4. Manage Your Time More Effectively: Time is a finite resource, and managing it wisely is crucial for personal and professional success. By using time management techniques, such as prioritization, delegation, and time blocking, you can make the most of your time and achieve more in less time. You'll learn time management

techniques and how to prioritize tasks to improve your productivity.

5. Practice Self-Care: Self-care refers to activities and practices that promote physical, mental, and emotional well-being. By taking care of yourself, you can reduce stress, improve your mood, and enhance your overall quality of life. You'll learn the importance of self-care and how to incorporate it into your daily routine.

6. Build Stronger Relationships: Relationships are an essential aspect of life, and building positive relationships with others is crucial for personal and professional success. By improving your communication skills, practicing empathy, and building trust, you can foster meaningful connections with others. You'll learn how to communicate

effectively and build positive relationships with others.

7. Continue To Learn And Grow: Lifelong learning is the key to personal and professional growth. By cultivating a love for learning and seeking out new knowledge and skills, you can stay relevant in your field, expand your horizons, and achieve your full potential. You'll learn how to cultivate a love for learning and continue to develop new skills and knowledge throughout your life.

Ultimately, this book is designed to help you become the best version of yourself and live a more fulfilling and purposeful life. By implementing the strategies outlined in this book, you can achieve your goals, improve your relationships, and live a happier and more meaningful life.

CHAPTER TWO

GOAL SETTING

Goal setting is an important aspect of personal development that involves setting specific, measurable, attainable, relevant, and time-bound (SMART) goals. Setting goals can help you stay focused, motivated, and accountable, and ultimately achieve success in your personal and professional life.

Here Are Some Tips For Effective Goal Setting:

1. Identify Your Long-Term Vision: Start by identifying your long-term vision for your life. What do you want to achieve in the next five or ten years? This will help you set meaningful and inspiring goals that are aligned with your vision.

2. Make Your Goals SMART: Make sure your goals are specific, measurable, attainable, relevant, and time-bound.

This will help you create clear and achievable goals that you can work towards.

3. Break down Your Goals: Break down your long-term goals into smaller, achievable milestones. This will make your goals more manageable and help you stay motivated as you work towards your long-term vision.

4. Write Down Your Goals: Writing down your goals can help you clarify them in your mind and make them more real. Write down your goals and review them regularly to keep them top of mind.

5. Share Your Goals: Sharing your goals with others can help you stay accountable and receive support and encouragement from others.

6. Track Your Progress: Track your progress towards your goals and celebrate your successes along the way.

This will help you stay motivated and focused as you work towards your long-term vision.

Remember, goal setting is an ongoing process. As you achieve your goals, you can set new ones and continue to grow and develop throughout your life.

THE IMPORTANCE OF SETTING GOALS

Setting goals is important for several reasons:

1. Provides Direction And Focus: Goals help you clarify what you want to achieve and provide a roadmap to get there. It provides a clear direction and focuses your efforts. They help you prioritize your time, effort, and resources towards the things that matter most, and steer you away from distractions or low-value activities. Without clear goals, it's easy to feel

aimless or uncertain about what you should be doing, which can lead to procrastination, burnout, or lack of progress.

2. Increases Motivation: Goals provide a sense of purpose and motivation to work towards something meaningful. It also provides a source of inspiration to work towards something that matters to you. When you have a clear goal in mind, you are more likely to put in the needed effort and be proactive, persistent, and resilient in the face of challenges or setbacks to achieve it. Goals also provide a sense of purpose and meaning, which can enhance your overall well-being and satisfaction with life.

3. Measures Progress: Goals provide a benchmark to measure progress and success. It provides a way to track your

progress and evaluate your success. By breaking down a long-term goal into smaller milestones, you can see tangible evidence of progress and build momentum over time. This can help you stay motivated and avoid feeling overwhelmed by a large, complex goal. Also, help you track your progress and make adjustments as needed to stay on track.

4. Boosts Confidence: Achieving goals boosts your confidence and self-esteem, as it shows you that you are capable of overcoming obstacles and achieving what you set out to do. Each small win along the way reinforces your sense of competence and progress, which can carry over to other areas of your life. Confidence is a key ingredient for success in any endeavour, whether personal or professional.

5. Promotes Personal Growth: Setting and achieving goals promotes personal growth and development, as it requires you to stretch beyond your current level of knowledge, skills, or abilities. It challenges you to step out of your comfort zone, learn new things, and develop new skills/competencies. The act of setting goals also requires self-reflection and introspection, which can help you clarify your values, beliefs, and priorities.

6. Enhances Focus And Productivity: Goals help you stay focused and productive, by providing a clear target to work towards. They help you avoid distractions or low-priority tasks, and prioritize your time and energy towards the most important tasks.

Overall, when you have a sense of direction and purpose, you are more likely to make progress and achieve your desired outcomes. Setting goals is essential for achieving success and personal growth. It provides direction, motivation, and a sense of purpose, and helps you stay focused, productive, and confident in your abilities. This will lead to a sense of satisfaction and fulfilment, which will enhance your overall well-being and happiness.

TYPES OF GOALS

There are several types of goals you can set for yourself, depending on the timeframe and scope of what you want to achieve.

Here are some common types of goals:

1. Short-Term Goals: These are goals that you can achieve within a few days, weeks, or months. These goals are typically smaller, more manageable steps that you can take towards a larger, long-term goal. They are often focused

on specific, immediate outcomes that you can achieve relatively quickly. Short-term goals are important because they can help you build momentum, maintain motivation, and track progress towards a larger goal. By breaking down a big goal into smaller, achievable steps, you can avoid feeling overwhelmed and stay focused on making progress. Examples of short-term goals might include completing a certain number of tasks each day, exercising for 30 minutes a day, reading a book a week, spending a certain amount of time practising a skill, or attending a networking event.

2. Long-Term Goals: These are goals that you want to achieve over a period of years. They are typically bigger, more complex goals that require significant effort, planning, and commitment over a

period of months or years. Long-term goals can be especially challenging to achieve because they require sustained effort and may involve overcoming significant obstacles or setbacks along the way. However, long-term goals can also be very rewarding, as they allow you to achieve something that is truly meaningful and significant. Examples of long-term goals might include owning a house, getting a degree, or starting a business.

3. Outcome Goals: These are goals that focus on achieving a specific outcome or result, such as winning a competition, achieving a certain level of income, or losing a certain amount of weight. Outcome goals are important because they provide a clear target to work towards, and can be very motivating. However, outcome goals can also be

challenging because they may be outside of your control or dependent on factors beyond your influence. To increase your chances of achieving an outcome goal, it's important to focus on the actions and behaviors that are within your control and to develop a plan for achieving the outcome you desire.

4. Process Goals: These are goals that focus on the actions or behaviours needed to achieve a desired outcome. Process goals are important because they help you identify the specific steps you need to take to achieve your goals, and can help you stay focused on the present moment rather than worrying about the future. Process goals are also useful because they allow you to track your progress and make adjustments as needed. Examples of process goals

might include spending a certain amount of time each day practicing a skill, writing a certain number of words each day towards a book, or saving a certain amount of money each month.

5. Performance Goals: These goals are focused on improving your performance or skills in a particular area. Performance goals can be especially useful if you are looking to achieve a specific level of proficiency or mastery in a skill or activity. Performance goals can also be helpful in providing a sense of achievement and recognition for your hard work and effort. Examples of performance goals might include running a certain distance in a certain amount of time, achieving a certain sales quota, or improving your public speaking skills.

6. Personal Development Goals: These are goals that focus on personal growth and self-improvement. It centers on improving yourself in some way, whether it's developing a new skill, building self-confidence, or cultivating a positive mindset. Personal development goals can be especially valuable because they can help you grow and evolve as a person, and can have a positive impact on many areas of your life. Examples of personal development goals might include improving communication skills, building self-confidence, or developing mindfulness practice.

Ultimately, the types of goals you set will depend on your priorities, values, and aspirations. It's important to have a mix of short-term and long-term goals, as well as outcome, process, and personal development goals, to ensure that you are making progress towards what matters most to you.

SMART GOALS

SMART goals are a framework for setting goals that are specific, measurable, achievable, relevant, and time-bound. The acronym **SMART** stands for:

> ➢ Specific: The goal should be clear and specific and focused on a particular area or outcome. When setting a specific goal, it's important to identify the exact outcome you want to achieve and to be clear on what steps you will need to take to get there. It should answer the questions of what, why, and how. For example, instead of setting a vague goal like "get in shape," you might set a specific goal like "lose 10 pounds in the next three months by exercising for 30

minutes per day and reducing my calorie intake by 500 calories per day."

➤ Measurable: A measurable goal is one that can be tracked and quantified in some way so that progress can be evaluated. This might involve setting concrete targets or milestones that can be used to assess or measure progress, such as "run a 5K in under 30 minutes" or "complete a project within a certain timeframe and budget."

➤ Achievable: An achievable goal should be challenging, but also realistic and attainable given your current resources and capabilities. This might involve breaking down a larger goal into smaller, more manageable steps, or identifying areas where you might need to develop new skills or resources in order to achieve your goal. It's important to ensure that the goal is not too easy, but also not so difficult that it becomes demotivating.

➢ Relevant: A relevant goal should be aligned with your overall personal development objectives and should be something that is important and meaningful to you. This helps to ensure that you are working towards something that is meaningful and important to you. This might involve reflecting on your values and priorities and identifying areas where you want to grow and develop.

➢ Time-bound: The goal should be time-bound, with a specific deadline or timeline for completion. This helps create a sense of urgency and helps keep you accountable for your goal. This might involve setting a specific date or timeframe for achieving your goal and identifying specific milestones or checkpoints along the way to track progress.

By using the SMART framework, you can ensure that your goals are well-defined, actionable, and designed to help you make meaningful progress towards your personal development objectives. This can help you stay focused, motivated, and on track towards achieving your desired outcomes.

HOW TO CREATE A PLAN TO ACHIEVE YOUR GOALS

Creating a plan to achieve your goals is an important step in making progress towards your personal development objectives. Here are some steps you can take to create a plan for achieving your goals:

1. Break down Your Goal into Smaller, More Manageable Steps: This step involves breaking your goal down into smaller, actionable steps that you can

take to move closer towards achieving it. Consider the specific actions you will need to take in order to achieve your goal and create a list or outline of these steps. You may also want to consider the order in which you will need to complete each step. This will help make the goal feel more achievable and less overwhelming.

2. Determine The Resources You Will Need: Think about the resources that you will need in order to achieve your goals, such as time, money, equipment, or support from others. Make a list of the resources you will need, and identify any potential barriers or obstacles that might need to be addressed.

3. Create A Timeline: Set specific deadlines for each step in the plan, and create a timeline for achieving your overall goal.

This helps create a sense of urgency and helps keep you on track. You may also want to consider incorporating specific milestones or checkpoints along the way to help you evaluate your progress.

4. Prioritize Your Tasks: Determine which tasks are most important, and prioritize them accordingly. This will help ensure that you are focusing your time and energy on the most critical steps towards achieving your goal. You may also want to consider the impact that each task will have on your overall goal, and prioritize the tasks that will have the greatest impact.

5. Identify Potential Challenges and Solutions: Think about potential challenges or obstacles that you might encounter along the way, and brainstorm possible solutions or strategies for overcoming them. This

helps you anticipate and prepare for potential roadblocks and increases your likelihood of success.

6. Track Your Progress: Regularly check in on your progress towards your goal, and make adjustments to the plan as needed. Celebrate your successes along the way, and use any setbacks or obstacles as opportunities to learn and grow. Consider keeping a journal or using a task management tool to help you track your progress and stay accountable to your plan.

By creating a plan to achieve your goals, you can break down your objectives into actionable steps and help ensure that you are making progress towards your personal development objectives.

Mack E. Rogas

CHAPTER THREE

MINDSET

Your mindset refers to your attitudes, beliefs, and thoughts that shape your behavior and actions. Developing a positive and growth-oriented mindset will help you improve your personal development and achieve your goals.

Here are some key aspects of mindset that you may want to consider:

➤ Fixed vs. Growth Mindset: A fixed mindset assumes that your abilities and traits are fixed and unchangeable, while a growth mindset believes that you can develop and improve your skills and qualities through effort and practice. Embracing a growth mindset can help you become more resilient and open to learning and growth.

➢ Positive vs. Negative Mindset: Your mindset can also be categorized as positive or negative based on your overall attitude towards yourself and the world around you. A positive mindset emphasizes optimism, gratitude, and abundance, while a negative mindset focuses on pessimism, scarcity, and fear. Cultivating a positive mindset can help you feel more motivated and energized, while a negative mindset can drain your energy and limit your potential.

➢ Self-Limiting Beliefs: Your mindset can be influenced by self-limiting beliefs, which are negative or untrue thoughts that hold you back from achieving your goals. Common self-limiting beliefs include "I'm not good enough" or "I'll never be able to do that." Identifying and challenging your self-limiting beliefs can help you overcome them and develop a more positive and growth-oriented mindset.

➢ Mindfulness: Mindfulness is the practice of being present and aware in the current moment, without judgment. Mindfulness can help you become more aware of your thoughts and emotions, and develop a more positive and compassionate mindset towards yourself and others.

➢ Positive Self-Talk: Your self-talk refers to the internal dialogue you have with yourself. Positive self-talk involves using affirmations and positive statements to reinforce positive beliefs and attitudes, while negative self-talk can reinforce self-limiting beliefs and negative attitudes. Practicing positive self-talk can help you develop a more positive and growth-oriented mindset.

By paying attention to your mindset and working to develop a positive and growth-oriented attitude, you can improve your personal development and achieve your goals.

THE POWER OF MINDSET IN PERSONAL DEVELOPMENT

Your mindset is a key factor in your personal development because it shapes your beliefs, attitudes, and behaviors. A positive and growth-oriented mindset can help you overcome obstacles, learn from mistakes, and achieve your goals, while a negative or fixed mindset can hold you back and limit your potential. By changing your mindset, you change the way you perceive yourself and the world around you, which leads to changes in your personal and professional life.

Here are some ways that mindset can impact your personal development:

1. Resilience: A growth mindset emphasizes the idea that challenges and setbacks are opportunities for growth and learning. This means that when you face obstacles, you are more likely to view them as opportunities to learn and improve, rather than as reasons to give up. When you have a growth mindset, you are also more likely to persevere in the face of challenges, and to bounce back from setbacks and failures.

2. Self-Awareness: A positive mindset emphasizes self-awareness and self-reflection. This means that you are more likely to be aware of your thoughts and beliefs, and to question any negative or self-limiting beliefs that might be holding you back. By being aware of your thoughts and beliefs, you can also

be more intentional about your actions and behaviors, which can help you achieve your goals.

3. Motivation: A positive mindset can help you stay motivated and focused on your goals, even when faced with obstacles or setbacks. When you have a positive mindset, you are more likely to believe in your ability to succeed and be optimistic about the future. This can help you stay motivated and engaged in your personal development, and can also help you overcome any self-doubt or negative self-talk that might be holding you back.

4. Growth and Development: A growth mindset emphasizes the idea that your skills and qualities can be developed and improved over time. This means that when you have a growth mindset, you are more likely to seek out

opportunities for learning and growth and to take risks and try new things. By embracing the idea that you can always improve and develop new skills, you are more likely to achieve your goals and succeed in your personal and professional life.

5. Positive Relationships: A positive mindset can also impact your relationships with others. When you have a positive mindset, you are more likely to be kind, compassionate, and empathetic towards others. This can help you build stronger and more positive relationships, which can in turn support your personal and professional growth.

Overall, the power of mindset in personal development lies in the idea that your beliefs and attitudes can shape your actions and behaviours. By cultivating a positive and growth-oriented mindset, you can improve your personal development, achieve your goals, and build stronger and more positive relationships with others. This involves being aware of your thoughts and beliefs, challenging self-limiting beliefs, and embracing the idea that challenges and setbacks are opportunities for growth and learning.

TYPES OF MINDSET

There are two main types of mindset that are commonly discussed in the context of personal development: the fixed mindset and the growth mindset.

➢ The Fixed Mindset: People with a fixed mindset believe that their abilities and traits are fixed and cannot be changed. They believe that their intelligence, talent, and personality are predetermined and that they cannot improve or develop these qualities. As a result, people with a fixed mindset often avoid challenges, feel threatened by criticism, and give up easily when faced with obstacles.

➢ The Growth Mindset: People with a growth mindset believe that their abilities and traits can be developed and improved through hard work, learning, and practice. They believe that they can improve their intelligence, talent, and personality over time and that failure and setbacks are opportunities for growth and learning. People with a growth mindset tend to embrace challenges, seek out feedback and criticism, and persist in the face of obstacles.

While fixed and growth mindsets are often discussed as distinct categories, it's important to note that most people exhibit a mixture of both mindsets in different areas of their lives. For example, someone might have a fixed mindset when it comes to their musical ability but a growth mindset when it comes to their public speaking skills.

It's also worth noting that mindset can be changed and developed over time with deliberate effort and practice. By cultivating a growth mindset, you will develop and improve your personal development, achieve your goals, and overcome any self-limiting beliefs or negative self-talk that might be holding you back in your personal and professional life.

HOW TO CULTIVATE A GROWTH MINDSET

Here are some strategies for cultivating a growth mindset:

1. Embrace Challenges: Instead of avoiding challenges, Seek out

opportunities that challenge you, even if they are outside of your comfort zone. Approach challenges with a positive attitude, viewing them as opportunities for growth and learning. Break big challenges down into smaller, manageable steps to avoid feeling overwhelmed.

2. View Failure as A Learning Opportunity: Instead of seeing failure as a reflection of your innate abilities, see it as a necessary part of the learning process also, as an opportunity to learn and improve. Analyze what went wrong, ask yourself what you can learn from the experience and how you can use that knowledge to do better in the future. Recognize that every failure is an opportunity to learn and grow.

3. Focus On the Process, Not Just the Outcome: Instead of solely focusing on

achieving a specific outcome or result, focus on the steps and processes you need to take to get there. Celebrate progress and small successes along the way, even if you haven't achieved your ultimate goal yet. Break your goals down into smaller, more manageable steps. Reflect on the progress you have made, and use it as motivation to keep going.

4. Cultivate A Learning Mindset: Embrace a love of learning and seek out new challenges and opportunities that will help you learn and grow. Whether it's through taking classes, reading books, attending workshops or been open to feedback, constructive criticism, and advice from others, prioritize ongoing learning and development to expand your knowledge and skills.

5. Reframe Negative Self-Talk: Instead of letting negative self-talk hold you back, reframe your inner dialogue in more positive and empowering ways. For example, instead of thinking; I'm not good enough, reframe it to; I am capable of improving and growing. Practice self-compassion and be kind to yourself, especially when things don't go as planned.

6. Surround Yourself With Growth-Oriented People: Surround yourself with people who inspire and encourage you to grow and develop. Seek out mentors and role models who embody a growth mindset, and avoid people who discourage or belittle your efforts to improve.

Remember, cultivating a growth mindset is a journey, not a destination. It takes time, effort, and practice to shift from a fixed mindset to a growth mindset. But by consistently practising these strategies, you can overcome self-limiting beliefs and achieve greater success and fulfilment in your personal and professional life.

TIPS FOR OVERCOMING LIMITING BELIEFS

Here are some tips for overcoming limiting beliefs:

1. Identify Your Limiting Beliefs: The first step in overcoming limiting beliefs is to become aware of the negative thoughts or beliefs. Pay attention to negative self-talk and the thoughts that hold you back. Write them down and ask yourself where they come from. Are they based on past experiences or fear of failure?

2. Challenge your Limiting Beliefs: Once you've identified your limiting beliefs, challenge them with evidence to the

contrary. Look for examples of people who have succeeded despite similar circumstances, or examine times when you have overcome similar obstacles in the past. Ask yourself whether your limiting belief is really true or if it's just something you've accepted without questioning it.

3. Reframe Your Beliefs: Instead of focusing on what you can't do, reframe your beliefs to focus on what you can do. Use positive affirmations to reinforce your new beliefs. For example, instead of telling yourself "I'm not good enough," try telling yourself "I'm capable of learning and growing."

4. Surround Yourself With Positive Influences: Surround yourself with people who support your growth and development. Seek out mentors or role models who can help you overcome

your limiting beliefs. Be mindful of the negative influences in your life and try to limit your exposure to them.

5. Take Action: One of the most effective ways to overcome limiting beliefs is to take action in spite of them. Focus on what you can do today to move forward, even if it's just taking small steps. This will help you build confidence and momentum.

6. Practice Self-Compassion: Be kind to yourself and acknowledge that it's normal to have limiting beliefs. Practice self-compassion and forgive yourself for past mistakes or failures. Treat yourself as you would treat a friend who is struggling.

7. Seek Help If Needed: If you're struggling to overcome your limiting beliefs, don't be afraid to seek help from a therapist or coach. They can help you

identify and challenge your beliefs and develop strategies to overcome them. Remember that seeking help is a sign of strength, not weakness.

Remember that overcoming limiting beliefs is a process that takes time and effort. But by consistently challenging your beliefs and taking action, you can break through self-imposed barriers and achieve your goals. Be patient with yourself and celebrate your progress along the way.

Mack E. Rogas

CHAPTER FOUR

TIME MANAGEMENT

Time management is the process of planning and organizing how much time you spend on specific tasks and activities to increase efficiency and productivity. Effective time management skills are essential for personal and professional success. It involves setting priorities, delegating tasks, and managing your time effectively to meet your goals.

Some Tips for Improving Your Time Management Skills:

➤ Prioritize Tasks: Prioritizing tasks involves identifying the most important tasks and completing them first. Make a to-do list and categorize tasks according to their level of importance and urgency.

➤ Set Goals: Setting goals can help you stay focused and motivated. Create specific, measurable, achievable, relevant, and time-bound (SMART) goals that align with your overall objectives.

➢ Manage Distractions: Distractions can be a significant obstacle to effective time management. Try to identify the things that distract you and minimize or eliminate them. For example, turn off notifications on your phone or block distracting websites during work hours.

➢ Use a Calendar or Planner: A calendar or planner can help you stay organized and on track. Use it to schedule your tasks, appointments, and deadlines. You can also set reminders to help you stay on top of your schedule.

➢ Delegate Tasks: Delegating tasks involves assigning some of your responsibilities to others. Identify tasks that someone else can do and delegate them to free up time for more important tasks.

➤ Take Breaks: Taking breaks can help you stay focused and productive. Schedule short breaks throughout the day to recharge and avoid burnout.

➤ Learn To Say No: Saying no to non-essential tasks or activities can help you prioritize your time and focus on your goals.

By implementing these time management strategies, you can improve your productivity, reduce stress, and achieve your goals more effectively. Remember that time management is an ongoing process and requires continuous effort and practice to be successful.

Mack E. Rogas

THE IMPORTANCE OF TIME MANAGEMENT IN PERSONAL DEVELOPMENT

Effective time management is a critical aspect of personal development because it helps individuals achieve their goals, increase productivity, reduce stress, and improve overall well-being. Here are some specific reasons why time management is important in personal development:

1. Achieving Goals: Time management is essential for achieving personal and professional goals. Without effective time management, it is easy to get sidetracked by less important tasks and lose sight of your priorities. By setting priorities and managing your time effectively, you can focus on tasks that are most important and work towards achieving your goals efficiently. For

example, you may set aside a specific time each day to work on a project, rather than allowing yourself to get distracted by other tasks.

2. Increased Productivity: Good time management skills can help you be more productive by maximizing the amount of work you can complete in a given time period. By prioritizing tasks and managing distractions, you can work more efficiently and get more done in less time. For example, you may set specific times each day to check emails or return phone calls, rather than allowing yourself to be constantly interrupted by notifications.

3. Reduced Stress: Poor time management can lead to stress and overwhelm, as individuals struggle to balance their workload with other responsibilities. By managing your time effectively, you can

reduce stress levels and feel more in control of your workload. For example, you may set specific times each day to work on tasks, and take breaks throughout the day to rest and recharge.

4. Improved Well-Being: Time management skills can help individuals achieve a healthy work-life balance. By prioritizing tasks and taking breaks when necessary, you can maintain good physical and mental health and avoid burnout. For example, you may schedule time each day for exercise, socializing, or other hobbies to help maintain balance in your life.

5. Professional Success: Effective time management is crucial for professional success. By being organized and efficient, you can impress employers and colleagues with your productivity and work towards achieving career

goals. For example, you may use time management tools such as calendars or to-do lists to prioritize tasks and ensure that deadlines are met.

In summary, time management is an important component of personal development as it helps individuals achieve their goals, increase productivity, reduce stress, and improve overall well-being.

HOW TO PRIORITIZE TASKS

Prioritizing tasks is an important part of effective time management. Here are some steps you can take to prioritize tasks:

1. Make a To-Do List: Start by making a list of all the tasks you need to complete. This includes both work-related tasks and personal tasks. This can help you see the big picture and ensure that nothing is forgotten.

2. Identify Urgent and Important Tasks: Go through your list and identify which tasks are urgent and which are important. Urgent tasks are those that need to be done immediately, while important tasks are those that have a significant impact on your goals or objectives. Urgent tasks might include responding to an email from your boss or meeting a tight deadline, while important tasks might include working on a long-term project or developing a new skill.

3. Use the Eisenhower Matrix: The Eisenhower Matrix is a popular tool for prioritizing tasks. The Eisenhower Matrix is a four-quadrant grid that helps you categorize tasks based on their level of urgency and importance. Draw a square and divide it into four quadrants. Label the first quadrant "Urgent and

Important," the second quadrant "Important but not Urgent," the third quadrant "Urgent but not Important," and the fourth quadrant "Not Urgent and not Important."

i. Urgent and Important: These tasks should be done first and given the highest priority.

ii. Important but Not Urgent: These tasks should be scheduled and given a specific deadline.

iii. Urgent but Not Important: These tasks can be delegated or postponed.

iv. Not Urgent and Not Important: These tasks can be eliminated or put on hold.

4. Assign Tasks To The Quadrants: Go through your to-do list and assign each task to one of the four quadrants based on its level of urgency and importance.

For example, a task that is both urgent and important would be assigned to the "Urgent and Important" quadrant, while a task that is not urgent and not important would be assigned to the "Not Urgent and not Important" quadrant.

5. Prioritize Tasks: Once you have assigned each task to a quadrant, you can prioritize them based on their importance and urgency. Start with the tasks in the "Urgent and Important" quadrant, as these are the most critical tasks that need to be completed right away. Next, focus on the tasks in the "Important but not Urgent" quadrant, as these are important tasks that may not have a specific deadline but still need to be completed. Finally, look at the tasks in the "Urgent but not Important" quadrant, and consider whether they

can be delegated or postponed. Eliminate or put on hold tasks in the "Not Urgent and not Important" quadrant.

6. Consider deadlines: If a task has a specific deadline, make sure you prioritize it over other tasks that do not have a specific deadline. Even if a task is not urgent or important, it may need to be prioritized if it has a deadline.

7. Consider The Impact On Goals: Prioritize tasks that are directly related to your goals or objectives, as these will have the greatest impact on your success.

8. Be Flexible: Priorities can change over time, so it's important to remain flexible and adjust your priorities as needed. Regularly review your to-do list and Eisenhower Matrix to ensure that you

are staying on track and focusing on the most important tasks.

By prioritizing tasks, you can ensure that you are focusing on the most important and urgent tasks first, which can help you be more productive and achieve your goals more efficiently.

TIPS FOR AVOIDING PROCRASTINATION

Below are some tips for avoiding procrastination:

1. Break Tasks into Smaller Chunks: When you have a large task or project to complete, it can be overwhelming and easy to procrastinate. Breaking tasks into smaller, more manageable chunks makes them easier to approach and less overwhelming. This approach will make the task seem less daunting and more achievable. Also, helps you to focus on

one step at a time and feel a sense of accomplishment after each step. For example, if you have a project to complete, break it down into smaller tasks such as researching, outlining, and drafting.

2. Set deadlines: Setting deadlines for yourself provides motivation to get things done. Make sure you set realistic deadlines and stick to them. You can use tools such as calendars or productivity apps to help you keep track of your deadlines.

3. Use the Pomodoro Technique: The Pomodoro Technique is a time-management method that involves working for a set amount of time (usually 25 minutes) and then taking a short break. It involves breaking your workday into 25-minute work periods, followed by 5-minute breaks. After

every fourth work period, you take a longer break of 15-20 minutes. This technique helps you to stay focused during work periods, avoid procrastination and can improve your productivity.

4. Eliminate Distractions: Distractions such as social media notifications, phone calls, or email notifications can derail your productivity and cause procrastination. Turn off your phone or put it on airplane mode, close unnecessary tabs on your computer, and find a quiet place to work. Consider using noise-cancelling headphones if you are in a noisy environment.

5. Get Organized: A cluttered workspace or disorganized schedule can lead to procrastination, as it makes it difficult to find what you need and wastes time. Take some time to organize your

workspace and schedule, and make sure you have everything you need to complete your tasks. Use a planner or digital calendar to keep track of your schedule.

6. Use Positive Self-Talk: Negative self-talk can lead to procrastination and a lack of motivation. Instead, Use positive self-talk to motivate yourself and stay focused on your goals. For example, tell yourself "I can do this" or "I am making progress" to stay motivated.

7. Hold Yourself Accountable: Find someone to hold you accountable for completing your tasks. This can be a friend, coworker, or mentor who can check in with you regularly to make sure you are making progress. You can also use tools such as habit trackers or productivity apps to keep yourself

accountable. This will help you stay motivated and avoid procrastination.

Unlock Your Potential

CHAPTER FIVE

SELF-CARE

Self-care refers to the practice of taking care of one's physical, mental, and emotional health. It involves engaging in activities and behaviours that promote well-being and reduce stress. Self-care is important in personal development because it helps individuals maintain a healthy and balanced life.

TYPES OF SELF-CARE

1. Physical Self-Care: This type of self-care involves taking care of your physical health, including your body's basic needs. This includes getting enough sleep, eating nutritious foods, exercising regularly, staying hydrated, practicing good hygiene, and getting medical care when needed. By taking care of your physical health, you can improve your

energy levels, reduce stress, and promote overall well-being.

2. Emotional Self-Care: Emotional self-care involves activities that help you manage your emotions and maintain a positive mindset. This can include practising self-compassion, setting boundaries, journaling, talking with friends or a therapist, and engaging in activities that bring you joy. By taking care of your emotional well-being, you can improve your mood, reduce stress and anxiety, and build resilience to life's challenges.

3. Mental Self-Care: This type of self-care involves taking care of your cognitive health, including your ability to learn and process information. Examples of mental self-care include challenging yourself intellectually, learning new skills, practicing mindfulness or meditation, and engaging in hobbies or

activities that stimulate your mind. By taking care of your mental well-being, you can improve your focus, reduce stress, and promote overall cognitive function.

4. Spiritual Self-Care: Spiritual self-care involves practices that help you connect with your inner self or a higher power. This can include meditation, prayer, attending religious or spiritual services, spending time in nature, and practicing gratitude. By taking care of your spiritual well-being, you can cultivate a sense of inner peace, meaning, and purpose in your life.

5. Social Self-Care: Social self-care involves maintaining healthy relationships with others. This can include spending time with loved ones, making new friends, volunteering, and seeking support when needed. By taking care of your social

well-being, you can improve your overall happiness, reduce stress, and build a support system to help you through life's challenges.

Overall, practicing different types of self-care can help you create a sense of balance in your life, improve your overall well-being, and build resilience to life's challenges. It's important to find the self-care practices that work best for you and incorporate them into your routine regularly.

THE IMPORTANCE OF SELF-CARE IN PERSONAL DEVELOPMENT

Self-care is an essential component of personal development because it helps you maintain your physical, emotional, and mental well-being. When you prioritize self-care, you are better equipped to manage stress, maintain focus, and achieve your goals.

Below are a few specific ways that self-care benefit personal development:

1. Improved Mental Health: Engaging in self-care practices like meditation, exercise, and therapy can help you manage symptoms of anxiety, depression, and other mental health conditions. When your mental health is in good shape, you are better equipped to tackle personal development goals like learning a new skill or making a career change.

2. Increased Resilience: Self-care practices like exercise, meditation, and journaling can help you build resilience, which is the ability to adapt to stress and adversity. By building resilience, you are better equipped to handle setbacks and challenges that may arise as you

work towards your personal development goals.

3. Enhanced Productivity: When you prioritize self-care, you are better equipped to be productive and achieve your goals. Getting enough sleep, eating well, and engaging in physical activity can help you maintain your energy levels and focus, while activities like mindfulness and relaxation can help you manage stress and stay focused on your priorities.

4. Greater Self-Awareness: Self-care practices like journaling and meditation can help you become more self-aware and in tune with your thoughts, emotions, and behaviors. This increased self-awareness can help you identify areas for personal growth and development, and create a plan to achieve your goals.

5. Improved Relationships: Taking care of yourself can help you show up as your best self in your relationships with others. By managing stress, getting enough rest, and engaging in activities you enjoy, you are better equipped to be present and engaged with the people in your life.

In summary, self-care is a vital component of personal development because it helps you maintain your physical, emotional, and mental well-being, build resilience, enhance productivity, and increase self-awareness. By prioritizing self-care, you are better equipped to achieve your personal development goals and live a fulfilling, balanced life.

SELF-CARE ACTIVITIES TO START

Here are some examples of self-care activities you can start:

1. Physical Self-Care: Engaging in regular exercise boosts mood, reduce stress, and increase energy levels. Take a yoga class, go for a walk or run, get a massage, take a relaxing bath, or treat yourself to a healthy meal. Taking care of your physical health is an important part of overall self-care.

2. Emotional Self-Care: Emotions play a significant role in our well-being. Taking time to engage in activities that promote emotional well-being can help reduce stress, anxiety, and depression. Practice mindfulness meditation, write in a journal, spend time with friends and family, seek therapy or counseling, or engage in a creative hobby that you enjoy can provide a sense of comfort and support.

3. Intellectual Self-Care: Engaging in activities that challenge the mind can

help to promote cognitive function and overall well-being. Read a book or listen to a podcast on a topic that interests you, take a class or attend a workshop, learn a new skill or language, or engage in a challenging mental activity. This can help to expand your knowledge and understanding of the world around you.

4. Spiritual Self-Care: Spiritual self-care can help to provide a sense of inner peace and well-being. Practising gratitude, spending time in nature, attending a religious service or spiritual retreat, engaging in prayer or meditation, or participating in a mindfulness exercise can help to promote a sense of calm and tranquility.

5. Social Self-Care: Social support is an important aspect of overall well-being. Spending time with friends, loved ones or engaging in social activities can help

to reduce stress and improve mood. Joining a club or group that aligns with your interests, volunteer in your community, or attend social events or gatherings can also help to promote a sense of belonging and connection to others.

Remember, self-care is a personal and individualized practice, so it's important to find activities that work best for you and your need. Also, it's important to make self-care a priority in your daily life to promote overall well-being and personal development.

TIPS FOR CREATING A SELF-CARE ROUTINE

Below are some tips for creating a self-care routine:

1. Identify Your Needs: Take some time to reflect on what areas of your life need

attention and where you could benefit from self-care the most. This could include physical, emotional, social, or spiritual needs. Make a list of activities that could address those needs.

2. Make Time: It's easy to get caught up in the busyness of everyday life, but scheduling self-care time into your daily or weekly routine is essential. Treat it like any other important appointment or task. This means setting aside a specific time, turning off your phone or notifications, and dedicating your full attention to your self-care activity.

3. Set Boundaries: It's important to set boundaries to protect your self-care time. Learn to say no to commitments or obligations that don't align with your self-care needs. If you're having trouble saying no, remind yourself that you

can't take care of others if you don't take care of yourself first.

4. Experiment: Try different self-care activities and find what works best for you. Everyone's needs are different, so what works for someone else may not work for you. Try different activities and pay attention to how they make you feel.

5. Start Small: Don't overwhelm yourself by trying to do too much at once. Start with small self-care activities and build up to bigger ones. Even just a few minutes of deep breathing or stretching can make a big difference.

6. Be Consistent: Consistency is key when it comes to creating a self-care routine. Try to make self-care a regular part of your life, even when you're busy or stressed. Consistency can help you

establish healthy habits and make self-care feel more natural and effortless.

7. Be Kind To Yourself: Remember that self-care is about taking care of yourself and your needs. Be gentle with yourself and don't beat yourself up if you miss a self-care activity or routine. Just get back on track as soon as possible. Self-care is a journey, not a destination, so it's important to be patient and kind to yourself as you navigate it.

CHAPTER SIX

RELATIONSHIPS

Relationships are a crucial aspect of personal development. They can shape our perspectives, beliefs, values, and even self-esteem. Relationships can have a significant impact on our overall well-being, happiness, and success in life. Developing positive relationships can be a powerful tool for personal growth and development. In this chapter, we'll explore the importance of relationships, the different types of relationships, and how to cultivate healthy relationships for personal development.

Relationships can be defined as the way we interact with others, including our family, friends, colleagues, romantic partners, and even strangers. They can have a profound impact on our lives, influencing our thoughts, feelings, and behaviours. Positive relationships can provide emotional support, foster personal growth and development, and enhance our overall well-being. On the other hand, negative relationships can be detrimental to our mental and physical health, hinder our personal growth, and limit our potential.

There are different types of relationships, including familial, romantic, platonic, and professional. Each type of relationship has its unique characteristics, dynamics, and expectations. For instance, familial relationships are often based on blood ties and lifelong commitments, while romantic relationships are typically based on mutual attraction, intimacy, and emotional connection.

Cultivating healthy relationships involves building trust, communication, and respect. It requires actively listening to others, expressing empathy, and practicing forgiveness. By developing positive relationships, we can gain new perspectives, learn from others, and expand our social network. This, in turn, can lead to new opportunities for personal growth, self-discovery, and success in various areas of our lives.

THE IMPACT OF RELATIONSHIPS ON PERSONAL DEVELOPMENT

Relationships can have a significant impact on personal development. Positive relationships can provide emotional support, encouragement, and motivation, which can help individuals overcome obstacles and achieve their goals. They can also help individuals develop new skills, broaden their knowledge and perspectives, and promote personal growth.

On the other hand, negative relationships can hinder personal development by draining an individual's emotional energy, undermining their self-esteem, and limiting their potential. Negative relationships can create stress, anxiety, and depression, which can negatively affect an individual's mental and physical health.

Furthermore, the quality of our relationships can affect our overall well-being, including our mental and physical health. For example, studies have shown that individuals in positive relationships tend to have better mental health, lower stress levels, and higher levels of life satisfaction compared to those in negative relationships or those who are socially isolated.

In addition to the emotional and mental impacts of relationships on personal development, relationships can also impact an individual's social and professional development. For instance, positive relationships can provide networking opportunities, mentorship, and access to new resources that can help individuals advance in their careers.

Additionally, relationships can provide opportunities for personal learning and development. For example, working with a team on a project can help individuals develop their communication and collaboration skills, while conflict resolution in relationships can help individuals improve their problem-solving skills.

Moreover, relationships can also provide a sense of purpose and belonging, which can positively impact an individual's personal development. Feeling connected to others and having a sense of community can enhance an individual's self-esteem and confidence, which can promote personal growth and development.

In summary, relationships are a crucial aspect of personal development. Positive relationships can provide emotional support, promote personal growth, and enhance overall well-being, while negative relationships can hinder personal development and negatively affect mental and physical health. The impact of relationships on personal development is significant, and individuals should strive to build positive relationships that enhance their overall well-being and promote personal growth.

TYPES OF RELATIONSHIPS

There are various types of relationships that can impact personal development. Some common types include:

1. Romantic Relationships: These are intimate relationships between partners who have a romantic or sexual

connection. They are often characterized by strong emotional connections and a desire to spend time together. Romantic relationships can impact personal development by promoting self-awareness, communication skills, and empathy, while also providing emotional support and a sense of connection.

2. Family Relationships: These are relationships that are based on blood or legal ties, such as those between parents and children, siblings, or extended family members. These relationships are often characterized by shared history and a sense of obligation or duty. Family relationships can impact personal development by shaping an individual's values, beliefs, and behaviors, and providing emotional

support, guidance, and a sense of belonging.

3. Friendships: Friendships are non-romantic relationships between two or more people who share common interests, experiences, values, and hobbies. They are often characterized by mutual respect, trust, and support. Friendships can impact personal development by providing social support, enhancing communication and collaboration skills, and promoting personal growth through shared experiences and learning.

4. Professional Relationships: These are relationships that are based on a shared work or business-related context, such as those between coworkers, mentors, supervisors, employees and employers, or business partners. They are often

characterized by a focus on achieving common goals or objectives. Professional relationships can impact personal development by providing career guidance, mentorship, networking opportunities, and access to new resources and learning experiences.

5. Acquaintances: These are relationships with people who are known but not necessarily close friends or family members. They may involve occasional contact or communication, but they do not typically involve a strong emotional connection or ongoing commitment. Acquaintances can impact personal development by providing new perspectives, opportunities for learning, and potential networking connections.

Overall, each type of relationship can have a significant impact on personal development, as they all offer different opportunities for growth, learning, and connection with others, and it is important to build positive relationships across different spheres of life.

HOW TO BUILD POSITIVE RELATIONSHIPS

Building positive relationships is an essential aspect of personal development, it involves various elements that can contribute to establishing and maintaining healthy and meaningful connections with others. It can enhance emotional wellbeing, foster personal growth, and help achieve success in various areas of life. Here are some tips on how to build positive relationships:

1. Be Authentic: Authenticity is crucial in building positive relationships. It involves being genuine, honest, and true to oneself. People appreciate authenticity and are drawn to those who are real and transparent.

2. Building Trust: Trust is a critical component of any relationship. It is built through consistent actions that show dependability, reliability, and honesty.

3. Effective Communication: Good communication is key to building positive relationships. It involves being an active listener, expressing oneself clearly and respectfully, and being open and honest in one's communication. Good communication skills help foster understanding, empathy, and respect.

4. Empathy: Empathy is the ability to understand and share the feelings of others. It helps build positive relationships by promoting understanding, trust, and respect.

5. Positive Attitude: A positive attitude can help build positive relationships. It involves being optimistic, having a can-

do attitude, and seeing the best in others.

6. Mutual Respect: Mutual respect is vital in building positive relationships. It involves acknowledging and valuing the differences and perspectives of others. Also, treating others with dignity, kindness, and consideration.

7. Setting Boundaries: Boundaries help to define what is and is not acceptable in a relationship. It is important to set boundaries and communicate them clearly to ensure that both parties feel comfortable and respected.

8. Shared Interests: Shared interests and hobbies can help build positive relationships and create a sense of connection and enjoyment in a relationship. Participating in activities with others who share similar interests can deepen bonds, create a sense of

community and foster connections through positive memories.

9. Giving and Receiving Support: Support is crucial in any relationship, whether it involves emotional support during tough times or practical help with daily tasks. It is important to both give and receive support to build trust and foster a sense of reciprocity.

10. Quality Time: Spending quality time with others can help build positive relationships. It involves giving others undivided attention, being present, and creating memorable experiences together.

11. Managing Conflicts: Conflict is a natural part of any relationship, but learning to manage it constructively is essential for building positive relationships. Effective conflict management involves active listening, expressing oneself assertively,

and seeking to find solutions that work for everyone involved.

Remember that building positive relationships takes time and effort, but the rewards are immeasurable. Positive relationships can enrich our lives, help us grow as individuals, and enhance our overall sense of wellbeing which contribute to personal growth and development.

TIPS FOR SETTING BOUNDARIES IN RELATIONSHIPS

Setting boundaries is an important aspect of building healthy and positive relationships. Here are some tips for setting boundaries in relationships:

1. Identify Your Boundaries: The first step in setting boundaries is to identify your boundaries. What are your limits and

what behaviours or actions make you uncomfortable? Be clear about what you will and will not accept in your relationships. Be honest with yourself and make a list of your boundaries.

2. Communicate Your Boundaries: Once you have identified your boundaries, it is important to communicate them clearly and assertively to the people in your life. Be firm, and respectful when communicating your boundaries.

3. Be Consistent: It is important to be consistent in enforcing your boundaries. If you set a boundary with someone, make sure you stick to it. This will help establish a pattern of behavior and create a sense of predictability in your relationships.

4. Practice Self-Care: Setting boundaries can be difficult, especially if you are used to people-pleasing or prioritizing

others over yourself. To maintain healthy boundaries, it's important to practice self-care regularly. Take care of yourself physically, emotionally, and mentally so that you have the strength and energy to maintain your boundaries. This could include exercise, meditation, or spending time doing something you enjoy.

5. Seek Support: Setting boundaries can be challenging, so it is important to seek support from friends, family, or a therapist. Having support can help you stay strong in enforcing your boundaries.

6. Be Prepared For Pushback: Setting boundaries can sometimes lead to pushback or resistance from others. Be prepared to stand firm in your boundaries and communicate your needs clearly. Remember that setting

boundaries is a healthy way to take care of yourself, and it's important to prioritize your well-being.

Overall, setting boundaries is an important part of building positive relationships. When you are clear about your boundaries, you create a sense of safety and predictability in your relationships, which can lead to increased trust and respect.

CHAPTER SEVEN

COMMUNICATION

Communication is the process of exchanging information, ideas, or thoughts between individuals or groups. In personal development, effective communication is essential for building positive relationships, setting and achieving goals, and expressing thoughts and emotions. Communication involves both verbal and nonverbal cues, such as body language, tone of voice, and facial expressions.

Effective communication requires both active listening and clear expression. It involves being able to understand the perspective of others while also conveying your own thoughts and feelings. Good communication skills can help improve personal and professional relationships, resolve conflicts, and build a sense of community.

Some Common Barriers To Effective Communication Include:

➢ Language Barriers: When people are speaking different languages or have different levels of proficiency in a shared language, it can be difficult to communicate effectively.

➢ Physical Barriers: This refers to the physical environment in which communication is taking place. It could be background noise, poor lighting, or even distance between the communicators.

➢ Emotional Barriers: People's emotional states can influence their ability to communicate effectively. For example, if someone is angry or upset, they may not be able to express themselves in a clear and calm manner.

➢ Cultural Barriers: Different cultures have different communication styles and norms. These differences can cause misunderstandings or even offense.

➤ Perceptual Barriers: This refers to differences in how people perceive things. For example, two people may interpret the same message differently due to their unique experiences and perspectives.

To improve communication skills, it is important to practice active listening, which involves paying attention to the speaker and responding in a way that shows understanding and empathy. Additionally, clear and concise expression can help to ensure that your message is understood and reduces the risk of misunderstandings.

Other Strategies For Improving Communication Skills Include:

➤ Being mindful of nonverbal cues, such as body language and tone of voice.

> ➢ Avoiding assumptions and clarifying misunderstandings.
> ➢ Practicing empathy and understanding the perspective of others.
> ➢ Using appropriate language and avoiding jargon or slang.
> ➢ Being respectful and avoiding interrupting or talking over others

By improving communication skills, individuals can build stronger relationships, resolve conflicts more effectively, and achieve personal and professional goals.

THE IMPORTANCE OF COMMUNICATION IN PERSONAL DEVELOPMENT

Effective communication is crucial for personal development as it allows individuals to express their thoughts, ideas, and emotions, and to understand others better. Communication helps people to build strong relationships, which in turn contributes to their emotional and mental well-being. When communication is lacking or ineffective, it can lead to misunderstandings, conflicts, and damaged relationships.

Communication is also important in achieving personal and professional goals. Effective communication skills enable individuals to articulate their ideas and goals clearly, persuade and influence others, and negotiate and resolve conflicts. It is an essential skill in various aspects of life, including personal relationships, work, and leadership.

Moreover, good communication skills are crucial in building self-confidence and self-esteem. When individuals can express themselves clearly and are understood by others, they feel more empowered and confident in their abilities. This self-assurance can lead to increased motivation, productivity, and success in achieving personal and professional goals.

TYPES OF COMMUNICATION

There are several types of communication, including:

1. Verbal Communication: This type of communication involves using words, either spoken or written, to convey a message. Verbal communication can take many forms, such as face-to-face conversations, phone calls, video calls, or presentations.

2. Nonverbal Communication: This type of communication involves conveying a message through body language, facial expressions, and gestures. Nonverbal communication can include things like tone of voice, posture, eye contact, and hand movements.

3. Written Communication: This type of communication involves using written words to convey a message. Written communication can take many forms, such as emails, letters, reports, memos, or social media posts.

4. Visual Communication: This type of communication involves using visual aids, such as images, videos, charts, or diagrams, to convey a message.

5. Digital Communication: This type of communication involves using electronic devices and platforms, such as email, social media, or instant messaging, to communicate with others.

6. Electronic Communication: This involves the use of electronic devices, such as computers, tablets, or smartphones, to communicate with others.

7. Interpersonal Communication: This is communication between two or more people and includes verbal and nonverbal communication.

8. Group Communication: This is communication that occurs within a group or team setting.

9. Mass Communication: This is communication that reaches a large audience through mediums such as television, radio, or social media.

HOW TO IMPROVE COMMUNICATION SKILLS

Improving communication skills involves developing a range of verbal, nonverbal, and written communication techniques that can help you to express your ideas, thoughts, and feelings clearly, effectively, and respectfully. Here are some tips for improving communication skills:

1. Listen Actively: Listening is an essential aspect of communication. Active listening involves paying attention to what the other person is saying, understanding their point of view, and responding appropriately.

2. Be Clear And Concise: When communicating, it is important to be clear and concise. Use simple language, avoid jargon or technical terms, and be direct in your communication.

3. Use Body Language: Body language can convey a lot of information about your feelings and intentions. Make eye contact, use gestures, and maintain an open and friendly posture to help create a positive and engaging interaction.

4. Practice Empathy: Empathy involves putting yourself in the other person's shoes and trying to understand their perspective. This can help to create a

more meaningful and respectful interaction.

5. Be Aware Of Cultural Differences: Cultural differences can affect communication styles and expectations. Be aware of these differences and try to adapt your communication style accordingly.

6. Give and Receive Feedback: Feedback is an important aspect of communication. Giving and receiving feedback can help to clarify expectations and improve the quality of communication.

7. Practice Active Speaking: Active speaking is about taking control of the conversation, being clear in your speech, and asking the right questions. This helps to ensure that your message is received and understood.

8. Use Technology Effectively: Technology has changed the way we communicate.

It is important to be familiar with different communication platforms and to use them effectively.

By implementing these tips, you will be able to improve your communication skills, which will in turn improve your personal and professional relationships, help you achieve your goals, and enhance your overall personal development.

TIPS FOR EFFECTIVE COMMUNICATION

Below are some tips for effective communication:

1. Listen Actively: To communicate effectively, you need to listen to the other person actively. This means giving your full attention to the speaker. Focus on what the person is saying, rather than thinking about your response. Ask clarifying questions if you are unsure

about something they said, and summarize what you heard to ensure you understand correctly.

2. Be Clear And Concise: When communicating, be clear and concise in your message. Use simple language and try to convey your message in a way that is easy to understand. Avoid using jargon or technical terms that the other person may not be familiar with.

3. Use Non-Verbal Communication: This includes things like body language, facial expressions, and tone of voice. These can often convey more information than words alone. Be aware of your own non-verbal communication, make sure it aligns with your words and try to read the non-verbal cues of the person you are communicating with. Maintain eye contact, use appropriate

facial expressions, and avoid slouching or crossing your arms.

4. Be Empathetic: Empathy is the ability to understand and share the feelings of another person. It's important to be empathetic when communicating with others, especially in situations where emotions are involved. Try to put yourself in their shoes and understand their perspective. This will help you communicate in a more compassionate and understanding way.

5. Be Open-Minded: Avoid making assumptions or jumping to conclusions. Keep an open mind and be willing to consider other perspectives.

6. Avoid Assumptions: Don't assume that the other person understands what you are saying or what you mean. Clarify your message and make sure that you are both on the same page. Similarly,

avoid making assumptions about the other person's thoughts or feelings.

7. Avoid Distractions: When communicating, avoid distractions such as checking your phone or watching TV. Focus on the conversation and give it your full attention.

8. Provide Feedback: When communicating, provide feedback to the other person to ensure you both are on the same page. Ask questions, summarize your understanding, and acknowledge the other person's perspective.

9. Be Respectful: Respect is an important part of effective communication. Always communicate in a respectful manner. Treat the other person with respect and avoid using aggressive or confrontational language. Avoid interrupting, belittling, or talking over

the other person. Use "I" statements instead of "you" statements to avoid putting the other person on the defensive. Treat them with kindness and consideration.

10. Practice Active Constructive Responding: Active Constructive Responding (ACR) is a technique for responding to positive news from others. Instead of simply saying "that's great," actively engage with the person and show your enthusiasm. This can help build stronger relationships and increase positive emotions.

By following these tips, you can improve your communication skills and become a more effective communicator in your personal and professional life.

CHAPTER EIGHT

CONTINUOUS LEARNING

Continuous learning refers to the process of acquiring knowledge, skills, and expertise throughout one's life. It involves actively seeking out new information, developing new skills, and staying current with the latest trends and developments in one's field.

Continuous learning is essential for personal development because it allows individuals to stay relevant and competitive in their careers, adapt to changing circumstances, and pursue new opportunities. It also fosters personal growth, enhances problem-solving skills, and helps individuals become more well-rounded and informed.

There are many ways to engage in continuous learning, including formal education, online courses, workshops, mentorship programs, and self-directed learning. The key is to have a growth mindset and a willingness to learn and explore new things.

Continuous learning also helps individuals develop a growth mindset, which is the belief that one's abilities and intelligence can be developed through hard work, dedication, and persistence. This mindset encourages individuals to embrace challenges and view failures as opportunities to learn and grow.

THE IMPORTANCE OF CONTINUOUS LEARNING IN PERSONAL DEVELOPMENT

Continuous learning is essential for personal development because firstly, it helps individuals stay relevant and adaptable in a rapidly changing world. With new technologies, ideas, and knowledge emerging at a rapid pace, it is critical to stay up-to-date and learn new skills to remain competitive in the job market. Secondly, continuous learning also allows individuals to develop a growth mindset and a desire for self-improvement. Learning new skills and acquiring knowledge can enhance confidence and self-esteem leading to greater personal satisfaction and a sense of achievement. Thirdly, it can improve cognitive function, enhance problem-solving skills, and increase creativity and innovation. Lastly, continuous learning can open up new opportunities for personal and professional growth, as well as lead to greater financial rewards.

Furthermore, continuous learning is essential for adapting to change, which is an inevitable part of life. The ability to learn and adapt to new circumstances can help individuals overcome challenges and obstacles they may encounter. It also allows them to be more resilient in the face of adversity and develop a growth mindset.

In addition, continuous learning can be a source of personal fulfillment and enjoyment. Learning new things can be an enriching experience, providing individuals with a sense of intellectual curiosity and a desire to explore new subjects and ideas.

Overall, continuous learning is critical for personal development as it provides individuals with the skills, knowledge, and mindset necessary to succeed and thrive to achieve their full potential and lead a fulfilling life both in their personal and professional lives.

TYPES OF LEARNING

There are several types of learning, including:

1. Formal Learning: Formal learning refers to structured learning that takes place in a formal setting such as a classroom, training program, or workshop. It typically follows a pre-determined

curriculum and is delivered by a teacher, instructor, or trainer and may result in a degree, certificate, or other type of credential. Examples of formal learning include attending college or university, professional development courses, and certificate programs.

2. Informal Learning: Informal learning is the type of learning that occurs outside of a formal setting or structured environment, such as learning from experience or observing others. It is self-directed and can be intentional or unintentional. Informal learning can occur through daily life experiences, social interactions, reading, watching videos, or attending workshops. It may not result in a formal credential, but can be just as valuable as formal learning. Examples of informal learning include learning how to cook from a friend,

attending a networking event, or learning a new skill through a YouTube tutorial.

3. Non-Formal Learning: Non-formal learning is a type of structured learning that takes place outside the formal education system. It is organized and can be targeted to specific groups or individuals, but without the intention of obtaining a formal credential. Examples include after-school programs, adult education courses workshops, seminars, and short courses.

4. Experiential Learning: Experiential learning is a type of learning that involves learning by doing. This occurs through direct experience, such as on-the-job training or volunteering. It is a hands-on approach to learning that enables individuals to apply theoretical knowledge to real-world situations.

Examples of experiential learning include internships, apprenticeships, field trips, and laboratory experiments.

5. Self-Directed Learning: This type of learning is initiated and directed by the learner, often through self-study or online courses. It involves taking responsibility for one's own learning, identifying learning goals, and developing strategies to achieve them. Examples of self-directed learning include learning a new language, reading books on a specific topic, or taking online courses.

6. Collaborative Learning: This type of learning occurs through group activities or projects, and involves working with others to achieve a common goal.

7. Blended Learning: Blended learning is a type of learning that combines different types of learning, such as formal and

informal learning, to create a holistic learning experience. Blended learning can take place in the classroom or online and involves a combination of lectures, group work, discussions, and online resources.

HOW TO CULTIVATE A LOVE FOR LEARNING

Cultivating a love for learning can be a powerful tool for personal development. Here are some tips to help you develop a love for learning:

1. Find What You Are Interested In: Start by exploring topics that you find interesting or curious about. This will help you discover what you are passionate about and motivate you to learn more.

2. Make Learning A Habit: Dedicate a set time each day or week for learning

something new. Consistency is key when it comes to cultivating a love for learning.

3. Experiment with Different Learning Styles: There are many ways to learn, including reading, watching videos, attending classes, or listening to podcasts. Experiment with different styles to see what works best for you.

4. Join A Community Of Learners: Join a group or community of people who share your interests and are also passionate about learning. This can provide support, motivation, and opportunities for collaboration.

5. Set Goals and Track Progress: Set specific goals for what you want to learn and track your progress along the way. This can help you stay motivated and see the progress you are making.

6. Embrace Failure: Learning is not always easy and you will likely experience setbacks and failures along the way. Embrace these experiences as opportunities to learn and grow.

7. Keep An Open Mind: Be open to new ideas and perspectives. The more you learn, the more you will realize how much you do not know, and this can be a humbling and exciting experience.

TIPS FOR LIFELONG LEARNING

Below are some tips for lifelong learning:

1. Develop A Growth Mindset: A growth mindset involves embracing challenges and seeing failures as opportunities for growth rather than as setbacks. When you have a growth mindset, you are more likely to be open to learning and to see the value in continuous learning.

2. Pursue Your Interests: Focus on learning about topics that you are genuinely interested in, as this will keep you motivated and engaged in the learning process.

3. Set Learning Goals: Setting specific learning goals can help you stay focused and motivated. These goals can be big or small, short-term or long-term, and they should be realistic and achievable. It can be reading a certain number of books per month or mastering a new skill.

4. Create A Learning Plan: Once you have set your learning goals, it's important to create a plan that outlines the steps you will take to achieve them. This can include identifying resources, setting a timeline, and breaking down larger goals into smaller, more manageable tasks. Incorporate learning into your

daily routine, whether it's reading a book for 30 minutes before bed or listening to a podcast on your commute to work.

5. Embrace A Variety Of Learning Methods: Everyone learns differently, so it's important to embrace a variety of learning methods. This can include reading, listening to podcasts, watching videos, attending workshops or classes, and engaging in hands-on learning experiences.

6. Engage In Active Learning: Active learning involves actively engaging with the material you are learning rather than simply passively absorbing it. This can involve asking questions, making connections to your own experiences, and applying what you have learned to real-world situations.

7. Stay Curious: Approach new experiences and challenges with an open mind and a willingness to learn. Stay curious about the world around you.

8. Embrace Failure: Don't be afraid to fail or make mistakes. Instead, see them as opportunities for growth and learning.

9. Find A Learning Community: Learning with others can be a great way to stay motivated and gain new perspectives. Consider joining a book club, taking a class, or finding a mentor or coach who can support your learning journey.

10. Seek Out Mentors And Teachers: Look for people who can offer guidance and support in your learning journey. This can be in the form of a mentor, coach, or teacher.

11. Use Technology: Take advantage of online courses, tutorials, and other

learning resources available through technology.

12. Stay Organized: Keep track of your progress and learning materials in a way that works for you. This can be through note-taking, journaling, or using an app.

13. Stay Accountable: Share your learning goals with others and seek their support and encouragement. This can help keep you accountable and motivated to continue learning.

14. Reflect On Your Learning: Take time to reflect on what you have learned and how it can be applied to your life. This can help solidify your new knowledge and help you identify areas where you may need further growth or development. This can include journaling, discussing your learning with others, or simply taking time to

pause and think about what you have learned.

CHAPTER NINE

CONCLUSION

Personal development is an ongoing process that requires intentional effort, discipline, and a growth mindset. By adopting a growth mindset, prioritizing time management, practising self-care, building positive relationships, improving communication skills, and engaging in continuous learning, individuals can enhance their personal development journey. It involves taking the time to reflect on oneself, setting goals, and taking action to achieve those goals. The five key areas of personal development - mindset, time management, self-care, relationships, and communication - are all interconnected and play an important role in an individual's growth and success. By focusing on these areas and implementing the tips and strategies discussed, individuals can create a fulfilling and meaningful life. Continuous learning is also an important aspect of personal development, as it allows individuals to acquire new skills and knowledge, stay up-to-date with the latest trends, and adapt to changing circumstances. By making personal development a priority, individuals can unlock their full potential and live their best life.

RECAP OF KEY POINTS

A recap of the key points covered in this book will be:

Personal development involves improving oneself in various areas of life such as mindset, time management, self-care, relationships, communication, and continuous learning.

A growth mindset, as opposed to a fixed mindset, is essential for personal development. Cultivating a growth mindset involves embracing challenges, learning from mistakes, and persisting through obstacles.

Prioritizing tasks and avoiding procrastination are crucial for effective time management. Steps for prioritizing tasks include listing tasks, identifying urgent tasks, and evaluating the importance of each task.

Self-care involves taking care of oneself physically, emotionally, spiritually, and mentally. Examples of self-care activities include getting enough sleep, eating well, practicing meditation, and engaging in hobbies.

Relationships have a significant impact on personal development. Building positive relationships involves being honest, empathetic, and supportive, and setting healthy boundaries.

Effective communication is essential for personal development. Barriers to communication include language barriers, cultural differences, and lack of listening skills. Improving communication skills involves being clear, concise, and empathetic.

Continuous learning involves consistently acquiring new knowledge and skills. Lifelong learning can be achieved through various methods, including formal education, informal learning, and experiential learning.

Overall, personal development involves taking proactive steps to improve oneself in various areas of life, with the goal of living a fulfilling and purposeful life.

ENCOURAGEMENT TO CONTINUE PERSONAL DEVELOPMENT JOURNEY

Remember that personal development is a lifelong journey, and there is always room for growth and improvement. Celebrate your successes, no matter how small, and don't be discouraged by setbacks. Keep pushing yourself outside of your comfort zone and trying new things. Surround yourself with supportive people who encourage and inspire you. And most importantly, be kind and patient with yourself, always stay open to learning and be willing to make changes to better yourself. With dedication and perseverance, you can achieve your personal development goals and live a fulfilling life.

RESOURCES FOR FURTHER LEARNING AND GROWTH.

There are numerous resources available for further learning and growth. Here are some suggestions:

Books: There are countless books on personal development, ranging from self-help to business and leadership. Some popular titles include "The 7 Habits of Highly Effective

People" by Stephen Covey, "The Ultimate Guide to Entrepreneurial Success" by Mack E. Rogas, "Mindset: The New Psychology of Success" by Carol Dweck, and "The Power of Now" by Eckhart Tolle.

Online Courses: Online learning platforms such as Coursera, edX, and Udemy offer a wide range of courses on personal development topics such as time management, leadership, and communication skills.

Coaches and Mentors: Hiring a coach or mentor can provide personalized guidance and support for your personal development journey. Look for someone who has experience in the areas you want to improve and has a coaching style that resonates with you.

Podcasts: Podcasts are a great way to learn and stay motivated while on the go. Some personal development podcasts to check out include "The Tony Robbins Podcast," "The School of Greatness with Lewis Howes," and "The Tim Ferriss Show."

Workshops and Seminars: Attending workshops and seminars can provide immersive learning experiences and opportunities to network with like-minded individuals. Look for events in your area or online that align with your personal development goals.

Remember that personal development is a lifelong journey, and there is always room for growth and improvement. Don't be afraid to explore new opportunities and try new things in your pursuit of personal growth.

www.ingramcontent.com/pod-product-compliance
Lightning Source LLC
Chambersburg PA
CBHW060845220526
45466CB00003B/1254